T0193284

THE GREEN PAPER RABBIT

KENRICK .L. GRANT

ILLUSTRATED BY TAIYE OKOH

The Green Paper Rabbit

To order additional copies of this book, contact:
Xlibris
844-714-8691
www.Xlibris.com
Orders@Xlibris.com

ISBN: Softcover   978-1-6698-2570-8
         EBook   978-1-6698-2569-2

Print information available on the last page

Rev. date: 05/03/2023

The Green Paper Rabbit

By

K. L. Grant

Tyson came in one day and said, "Dad, I want to get a bike. Can you give me the money?"

Tyson's dad said, "I would like to, but I don't have it. But I if you can figure out a way to get half of the money, I will give you the other half.

"You need to save your money first to get that bike."

Tyson thought about it for a while and said, "that's going to take me a long time."

"It might take time, but you can do it," Tyson's father replied.

"Can I get a bike too?" asked Tyson's little sister, Jada, playing with her dolls on the living room floor. Tyson's mother was listening to the conversation, and she suggested to Tyson to get a picture of the bike he wanted to put up on his wall to think about his goal to get the bike and how he could make it happen. Later that day, Tyson found a picture on the internet of the bike he wanted, printed it, and posted it on his bedroom wall.

The following day when Tyson woke, he asked his mom for half the money for the bike, but his mom knew that he wouldn't learn how to do things independently if she gave Tyson half the money.

Then Jada walked into the kitchen and asked her mom if she could help her bake some cookies so that they could sell them to earn enough money for the bike, "that's a great idea," yelled Tyson "we could sell the cookies, and I could get my bike." So, Tyson, Jada, and their mom took out all the ingredients and started to bake the cookies. The sweet smell of fresh-baked cookies filled the air down the street. "Ah, fresh-baked cookies," Tyson said as his mom pulled them out of the oven.

"Can I have one now?" Jada asked.

"When they cool down, you can take one," Jada's mom said, smiling "remember that they are there to help you get your bikes."

Tyson was so excited that he rushed to his room and grabbed some crayons and markers and a big piece of cardboard. "I'm going to make a sign so that we can put it in front of the house so that everyone can see it. Tyson and Jada drew and colored the sign and put up the table in front of the house. "Fresh homemade cookies for sale," the sign read. "Come get your fresh baked cookies," Tyson yelled as they waited patiently for customers to come to their stand.

Shortly after, an older gentleman came up to the stand, took out some money, and paid them for the cookies. Then the older man took out another dollar, but it was very crumpled up, and he also gave it to them. He said, "save this dollar. It is an exceptional dollar." As he pulled the money out of his pocket, the money landed on top of the cookie stand.

11

"It's a bunny rabbit," said Jada.

"It looks like a green paper rabbit," cried Tyson.

"Oh yes, it does," laughed the old man. "Well, look at the time. It's 5:32; remember the 50 30 20 rules, and you will be rich for the rest of your life."

"What are the 50 30 20 rules" inquired Tyson.

"It's the rules that we use to save your money, 50 percent of the money you use for your necessities, 30 percent you use for your wants, and 20 percent of your money you save for emergencies or long-term goals."

"What does that mean" asked Jada.

Oh, you will find out soon enough; ask the rabbit, said the old man as he strolled off.

Tyson took the green paper rabbit and put it in his pocket. Then he turned to Jada and said, "We will share him, we will keep him forever, he will be like our good luck charm." Jada nodded her head in agreement. They were thrilled that they had made their first sale. As the day wound down, they went inside to count the money they made on their cookie sale. "Mom, Dad, do you know about the 50 30 20 rules about money this old man told us about"? Tyson's parents looked at each other, very shocked.

"No, we don't; tell us what that means"? Tyson explained to them that it was a way of saving money for the things they wanted, and if they used those rules, they would be rich for the rest of their lives.

Later that night, as the children slept, the green paper rabbit jumped out of Tyson's pocket. Upon hearing the noise, it woke up Tyson.

"Oh, hello," said the green paper rabbit. "I didn't mean to disturb you and wake you up."

"What's going on," Jada said as she too woke up and saw the green paper rabbit.

"Well," said the green paper rabbit. "I didn't have time to do the things I wanted yesterday, so I thought I would get an early jump on things." As he looked at his watch, he said, "every morning at 5:32 before the sunrise; I would make sure that I have everything organized for the day. I get into a routine, just like you have a routine, you go to school, then come home and do your homework. I also have a routine where I go to work on my business.

"Why do you have to work on your business," asked Jada.

"I teach people and little children how to become financially independent, wealthy, and create generational wealth." Said the green paper rabbit.

"**H**ow do you do that"? asked Tyson

"I teach them techniques to save money and how to generate income streams." Did you know that you could save a lot of money by making a budget or clipping coupons before shopping?

"What's a budget?" asked Jada.

"A budget is the amount of money you allow yourself to spend every day or every week, and you don't go over that amount to reach your financial goals. Like the amount of money, you set to buy your bikes, you save for that and don't go over that amount."

Tyson and Jada looked confused, "you kids are young, and some of the things I will teach you, you might not have to worry about until you're older, but it is good for you to learn these things at an early age so you can put them into practice later in life. No matter how much money you make, you can always learn to save some, and that is why we use the 50 30 20 rules.

"I remember," Jada said, "the old man that gave you to us told us that."

The children went back to sleep and woke up early that morning; again, they looked at the pictures of the bikes they had hung on their bedroom walls.

They ate their breakfast, and once again, the children with their mom baked some more cookies. They quickly ran outside to put up the sign again for fresh-baked cookies. More people came to Jada and Tyson's cookie stand and bought all the cookies they had for sale.

"These are delicious," said one lady as she shoved the cookie in her mouth.

They are such young entrepreneurs, stated another lady as she ordered a dozen to bring home for her family.

After the kids sold all the cookies, they went back inside to check how much money they had made. "We did it this time," shouted Tyson as they went inside and counted the money, they had earned over the last two days of their cookie sale.

After counting the money, they divided the amount they needed for their bike and put the rest in a jar.

"What are you going to do with the extra money you made?" Tyson & Jada's mom asked.

"We do not know yet, but we want to put the rest up for an emergency, just in case we need to get our bikes fixed," they replied.

"That is excellent thinking," said Tyson and Jada's dad.

Later that week, Tyson and Jada went to the store with their father and bought the bikes they wanted.

Printed in the United States
by Baker & Taylor Publisher Services